SEEDS AND BLOSSOMS
HOW TO GROW A BEAUTIFUL LIFE

CHRISTINA LAM

BALBOA.
PRESS

A DIVISION OF HAY HOUSE

Balboa Press books may be ordered through booksellers or by contacting:

Balboa Press
A Division of Hay House
1663 Liberty Drive
Bloomington, IN 47403
www.balboapress.com
1 (877) 407-4847

Print information available on the last page.

ISBN: 978-1-9822-2386-1 (sc)
ISBN: 978-1-9822-2387-8 (e)

Balboa Press rev. date: 03/19/2019

ACKNOWLEDGMENTS

Dedicated to my beautiful children; Dannielle, Myles and Jamie whom they are my true teacher and guiding light in life.

CONTENTS

PROLOGUE

In 2016, I was in Glastonbury for a festival. Not the festival, I should say: this was a three day yoga festival: much more my cup of tea. You may or may not know that Glastonbury, besides the music festival, is famous for its spirituality. Ley lines and earth energies are said to surround the place, and myths and legends abound regarding the area's history. King Arthur is said to have visited in search of the Holy Grail, while Joseph of Arimathea is said to have brought the holy chalice – which was used at the last supper – to Glastonbury. Glastonbury Tor has even been described as the 'Isle of Avalon': the vale between this world and the next. In short, Glastonbury is a spiritual mecca.

On the final day of the festival, my daughter and I were lazing in the summer heat, resolved to spend the last day of our trip doing very little. Peacefully people watching, the sun warming our backs and the open fields and rolling hills of Glastonbury stretching as far as the eye could see, it was easy to see how those spiritual myths and legends might have begun, all those years ago, and why Glastonbury's reputation as the spiritual heart of the UK remained unchallenged, thousands of years later.

Of the people that we watched, one character in particular had caught my eye. Elona Woods, the sign beside her stall declaring her to be a clairvoyant and medium, had seemed to have an enormous queue for the duration of the festival. Not only that, but her customers seemed more than satisfied with the results of their readings. My daughter and I, more than a little sceptical, had been astonished to see customer after customer nodding enthusiastically at Elona, seemingly utterly convinced by her readings. 'How can people believe this stuff?' My daughter and I found ourselves saying again and again, as we watched yet another customer leave Elona's stall with tears in their eyes. Surely, we pondered, these people understood that so called psychics peddled their trade by spouting generic nonsense to vulnerable fools?

Eventually, as the crowds began to dwindle and most of the festival goers had headed home, curiosity got the better of me. Her queue had finally gone and, tentatively, I approached Elona.

'Are you free?' I found myself asking.

My daughter watched on, wearing a sceptically furrowed brow, as Elona asked me to sit down.

Her response had caught me off guard: I had expected her to tell me that she was about to pack up and head home herself. Instead, with no discussion of payment or whether or not I'd like a reading, I found myself sitting across from this mysterious clairvoyant as she pulled out tarot cards and, without asking me a single question, began to talk about my past and my future.

At first, I remained wary. Although many of Elona's comments about my past were accurate, I was sure that this must be a trick of the clairvoyant's trade, and although the wonderful predictions about my future were intriguing, they were of course impossible to verify, and I laughed them off politely. It was towards the end of the reading that something very strange happened. Elona looked me squarely in the eye and asked me a question.

'Did you know that you have an angel sitting on your shoulder, and his name is Gabriel?'

I felt a chill run over me, and goosebumps formed on my arms. I felt both touched and afraid and, as if from nowhere, began to cry. Once I had started, I couldn't stop: the tears ran down my cheeks like a river and, like the other customers that I had been so bemused by moments ago, I found myself nodding enthusiastically.

'Yes,' I told Elona. 'I do know it.'

In that instant I felt as though I had always known. I glanced over at my daughter - my cheeks still streaked with tears - and saw in her expression how baffled she was to see her mother become yet another duped customer. But the truth was, whether it was Elona Woods' insight or an epiphany of my own, I have always felt the presence of a guardian angel sitting on my shoulder. I have always known that if I want something from life, I need only ask for it, and it will materialise. As I sat across from Elona Woods and thought about all blessings that life has brought me – the opportunities, the experiences and the relationships – it was easy to believe that an angel had been guiding my path.

PART ONE

SEEDS

1

THE GOOD LIFE

In the years since that day at Glastonbury, life has continued to be sweet. Two years ago, at the age of forty-nine and three quarters, I retired from work. Those three quarters are worth mentioning: when I was thirty, my husband and I decided to set up our second business, and we were required to fill out all kinds of paperwork relating to finances and pensions. One of the questions we were asked was when we'd like to finish work. I thought about it briefly before replying:

'It'd be nice to retire a few months before I'm fifty... because fifty seems old.'

As I'm sure many of my fellow fifty-somethings will agree, fifty doesn't seem so old once you reach it! But I did indeed manage to retire at the age that I had hoped to – just one of the many instances in my life in which I have felt convinced that a guardian angel is guiding and protecting me. Perhaps Elona Woods had more insight than I had originally credited her with.

Although the word 'retirement' tends to be associated with peace and quiet, conjuring up images of people relaxing with their feet up, watching daytime television with a cup of tea in their hand, this has been far from my experience so far. Although I have been able to focus more of my time on personal goals and 'bucket list' experiences, I've certainly not spent much time with my feet up. If anything, things have felt busier.

In March of 2018, I finished a yoga course, the Level three Diploma in yoga teaching. This had been a long time goal and meant that I would be able to teach yoga to one-to-one or in a gym, but I was not yet qualified to teach in a yoga studio. In order to reach this stage, I would need to study more intensively – specifically, I would need 200 hours of yoga training. To do so, I spent September of 2018 in Italy with my yoga teacher, Ambra Vallo. Ambra is an enormous source of inspiration in my life: under her guidance, I completed a four week course which would normally be spread out over an entire year. Needless to say, it was an extremely challenging experience! By throwing myself into such an intense experience which took me so far beyond my comfort zone, I learned a great deal about my limitations and capabilities. I reached the end of the four weeks with not only an enormous sense of satisfaction but a qualification to teach in a yoga studio. Faye, the manager at my yoga centre back in Harborne, was quick to ask me to fill out an application form. However, after such a hectic four weeks, I felt I needed a break before hurtling forwards to the next step. After all, I had a few other goals to focus on first!

One of those goals was to expand my horizons in terms of travel. I had already ticked Zakynthos off of my list in August – I had long been beguiled by the 'party island' reputation of Zante, so when my husband and I visited we were sure to behave like rebellious teenagers, staying up until the early hours and listening to 'banging' house music. There were elements that our more mature status allowed us to focus on too though. The crystal clear turquoise of the Ionian Sea and the sweeping, rugged panoramas which surrounded us was truly breath-taking; the tranquillity of the landscape sharply contrasted with the frenetic mania of the partygoers on the Laganas strip and made the trip much more rewarding than I had ever dreamed it would be.

After spending September in Italy for the yoga course, I returned to England only briefly before heading back to the airport: this time I was with Jade Kuo, a long-time friend who I have known since my teens, and we were bound for Dubrovnik. While I had considered the Ionian Sea surrounding Zante to be beautiful, the waters of the Adriatic, which lap against the coast of Croatia, took beauty to a whole new level. It was like walking into a fairy tale.

November brought yet another trip: this time with my daughter. She and I headed to Nevada and Los Angeles for the trip of a lifetime. Before arriving, we were slightly apprehensive that Las Vegas might be nothing more than a hot spot for gamblers but we were happily proven wrong. Although neither of us bet a single penny, we took a great deal of pleasure in strolling up and down the various strips, taking in the bright lights and the neon signs. We even managed to attend a two day book writing course – one of the inspirations behind this project – and a Celine Dion concert!

We managed to tick off plenty of the touristic highlights of a visit to the west coast of the US: we saw the Hollywood sign, watched glamorous shoppers strutting through Beverley Hills, their arms laden with bags of designer clothes, and sampled the culinary delights of the Cheesecake Factory. It was utterly delicious, but I would advise anyone that visits to consider sharing a portion: as with everything we came across in America, my daughter and I were flabbergasted by the sheer vastness of our portions!

Perhaps the highlight of the trip was a helicopter ride in the Grand Canyon. When it comes to being amazed by vastness, nothing could compare to seeing the Grand Canyon with your own eyes. As we stopped for a picnic in the depths of the great crater, the sun blazing at our backs, I felt somewhat overwhelmed. It was a scene ripped straight from a travel catalogue, and one that I almost couldn't believe I was truly seeing for myself.

When I returned to the UK, I reflected on the fact that my life since 'retiring' had been akin to a mini-series – packed with excitement, drama and novelty. I decided that it was time to draw breath. After all, what was the point in taking on all of these new experiences if I couldn't find time to absorb and reflect?

It was in this state of reflectiveness that I found myself one morning, sat in my conservatory, notebook in hand. I looked out across the sweeping lawn of my beautiful garden and felt the pleasant tingle of the underfloor heating beneath my feet and felt quite overwhelmed. My horizons had not always felt this broad; my life had not always felt this abundant. It was not so much that my former self had not dared to dream of these things, but that she had not known that such things existed. In terms of geography, opportunity and happiness, I have come a long way in my five decades on earth.

I decided that it was time to look back: not just to reflect with gratitude on the blessings with which my life has been filled, but to see if there were any words of wisdom which I could pass on. My hope is that by sharing the events of my own life, as well as the attitudes that have shaped it and the lessons that it has taught me, those who find themselves reading these pages may benefit. I hope that by reading, you too might be able to find more joy and freedom in your own life, and that your happiness may blossom as mine has.

Yoga training with Ambra Vallo

Graduating as a yoga teacher in Italy.

2

BAREFOOT ON
THE BEACH

Throughout the first seven years of my life, I don't remember ever wearing shoes.

I'm not exaggerating! I grew up on Lantau Island, Hong Kong, in a small village called Big Wave Bay. I lived with my parents and three brothers – Alan, Tony and Kevin. Lantau is a small island and, although times have changed greatly in the decades since my childhood, back then it was far removed from the bustling metropolis for which Hong Kong is internationally recognised. We would visit it sometimes, to see our grandmother, but to do so required us to walk for twenty minutes, catch a bus and then take an hour long ferry ride before hopping on another bus once we reached the other side. In Lantau, life was simple. There were sixteen houses, simple in design, built in two neat rows of eight and facing onto a sandy beach. Everyone knew everyone, which meant that nobody ever locked their front doors. Most of our days were spent running around and playing on the beach. With a lifestyle like that, who would bother with shoes?

There were occasional interruptions to our simple routine of eat, sleep, beach, repeat. One instance of this was that from time to time, a supply teacher would visit the village. All of the children would be rounded up and taught something or other, all at once. Considering the fact that we ranged greatly in age (my siblings and I being the youngest and smallest in the village) and were not at all used to the classroom, I'm not sure how productive these lessons were! On other occasions, weekend tourists would make their way to Lantau to camp on the beach, hoping to soak up some of the village's serene atmosphere. Since our house was the nearest to the path, after dropping their bags off on the beach, these tourists would tend to knock on our front door and ask for some water to take down to the beach. We were utterly baffled by the intentions of these city dwelling visitors: what could possibly be so fascinating about Lantau that it was worth trekking all that way for?!

Our lifestyle was facilitated by the fact that my grandparents possessed a lot of farmland in Hong Kong. Besides a few chickens, pigs and cows, they owned land for growing rice, vegetables and peanuts, fields of peach trees and mountains dotted with pineapples. As grand as these assets may sound, we were not rich: money was quite limited and both of my parents needed to work to support us. My mother worked on the farm harvesting pineapples: to this day, I remember vividly the excitement of the arrival of the pineapple van. They would arrive early to the village, before sun rise, to collect huge straw baskets brimming with pineapples. It is a testament to the peace and tranquillity of my early childhood that the noise and excitement of the visits from the pineapple van registers to powerfully in my memory.

My father too worked on the farm, but also worked as a contractor, building roads and buildings all over Hong Kong. In particular, I recall him working on a government initiative in the 1970s, breaking up mountains to stretch land out into the sea. This work would demand a great deal of my father's time and energy, but this did not compromise my brothers and my respect for him. In spite of the pressure of his various responsibilities to the farm and to his family, I remember him as a warm and happy man. My fondest memories of him involve Alan, Tony, Kevin and I waiting at the top of the village for my father to return home from work: we would shriek with delight as he would lift all four of us at once – one on his shoulders, one on his back and another on each arm – and happily carry us all the way home.

In the village, we were well liked. Perhaps this was due to the respect that my father – always an honest and moral man, willing to help anyone – commanded. Perhaps it was my mother's reputation as a modern woman – a pretty young lady who had moved over from the 'big city' and thus exuded a mysterious and prestigious aura. Either way, our family was well known, well liked and our lifestyle was simple. This would all begin to change when I reached the age of seven and was sent to live with my grandmother to receive a more 'formal' education. But no matter what, I will always have those early memories of the village of Lantau, of days spent playing on the beach, and of a life where the height of drama was the early morning arrival of the pineapple van.

With my mum. A trip to the city to visit my Granma in HK.

3

STEPPING FOOT ON BRITISH SOIL

There is a great deal of truth in the saying that 'you don't know what you've got 'til it's gone'. Back in the late 1960s, my siblings and I took for granted that our simple beachfront life on Lantau Island was simply how life was and always would be. Unfortunately, the new decade brought with it various new regulations with regards to how farm land could be used and how products could be sold. Of course, being so young, my siblings and I didn't understand these complex factors ourselves. But our parents knew that they could no longer support our family through farming, so something would have to change.

An opportunity soon arose through my uncle Ho Tung, who had already moved to Staffordshire, England and ran a successful Chinese restaurant there. When my father informed my uncle of his struggles with the farm, my uncle applied for a work permit. The application was successful, and, although it would be two years before my brothers and I followed our parents, the next phase of my life had been set in motion: by 1975, I would move to England and become a second generation Chinese immigrant.

When we first arrived in Staffordshire, it felt as though we were aliens landing on the moon. It wasn't just the contrast of the much more urban lifestyle – we had already adjusted to this somewhat when living with our grandmother in Hong Kong. It was more that we were the only Chinese family in the area – the only foreign family, in fact – and so we stood out as extremely unusual and novel. Our alien status wasn't an entirely negative one though: although my brothers and male cousins recall weekly fights in the restaurant due to run-away unpaid bills, I personally have not experienced any violence at all as a child. Perhaps this was one of the blessings of being a girl!

Besides feelings of unusual and novel, my family and I felt very positive about our new life in the UK. People were mostly friendly and welcoming, and our new home seemed to us like the land of opportunity. My uncle had arrived with the mentality that if he worked hard, it would pay off. His work ethic was, frankly, incredible, and the success of his restaurant was a testament to his belief system. His inspirational attitude rubbed off on us all: a willingness to work hard in order to achieve your dreams soon became a core family value for us all.

It was at this time in my life, beginning primary school in Staffordshire, that my brothers and I began to learn English. I remember believing at the time that I knew nothing except how to speak English. It was both a blessing and a curse. The more I learned, the more I was able to make friends, settle into my new life and feel more like I belonged in the UK. But on the other hand, our increased fluency was not easily matched by our parents, and my brothers and I soon began to feel distant from our mother and father. Perhaps this was simply a natural consequence of our horizons – and our social circle – expanding so dramatically, but we began to spend less and less time with them, preferring the company of our English speaking school friends.

After working at my uncle's restaurant for a few years, my parents were at last ready to strike out and start a business of their own. This meant that – for the second time in my short life – I was to move away from a more rural life to start anew in the 'big city'. At the age of twelve, I was incredibly excited by the prospect of moving to somewhere – in my imagination, at least - as bustling and busy as Birmingham. In fact, it was something of a dream come true: we had visited on day trips, eating in seemingly exotic restaurants; to my mind, Birmingham was almost a holiday destination! It didn't matter to me – ignorant as I was at the time – that we were moving to the extremely deprived area of Small Heath. I was old enough to crave adventure but young enough to be unconcerned with issues such as social demographics.

As had been the case in Staffordshire, we were the only Chinese children to attend our school and the only Chinese family living in Small Heath. Unlike Staffordshire though, Small Heath was much more ethnically diverse. The area was predominantly populated by the South Asian community, and so we were no longer the only children for whom English was a second language, and the colour of our skin no longer made us stand out as aliens in a foreign land.

In the years that followed, my family and I moved around the Birmingham area a lot. It was difficult for my parents to establish themselves and their takeaway in Small Heath did not do well, after two years we had to move on. Consequently, it was necessary for us to move to wherever the work was. In the space of a few years, we lived in various flats and homes in Small Heath, West Bromwich and Selly Oak. I recall one particularly stressful day in which the business in Selly Oak was not survivable where we were required to move out of our home and be rehomed in a council flat. The precariousness of our situation – symbolised by the family being sat in our car with all of our worldly belongings, waiting for the council to find us somewhere new to sleep that night - remains seared in my memory. In spite of our financial difficulties and the constant change, my early teens were happy years. My horizons were small but I was satisfied with my lot, content to live day by day without worrying about my future prospects. Although all my siblings were male and were developing different interests to me, I didn't struggle to occupy myself during my free time. I would receive £3 a week in pocket money, all of which I would splurge on magazines – issue after issue of Pop Magazine and Tammy – and vinyl records, despite the fact that I had no device on which to play them!

Happily, I became popular at school. I was drawn to the trendiest and toughest girls in my year group which meant that, in spite of my tiny stature, I was never picked on or bullied. Regardless, I often bemoaned my smallness and longed to be taller. One day though, a friend of mine, Annette, told me not to worry, reminding me that 'precious stones come in small boxes'. It was such a throwaway line, but I have carried it with me to this day. It is funny to think how the tiniest moments can carry so much weight, but the experience seems, to me, to carry an important lesson regarding the power of words. The positivity of this 'mantra' from Annette has allowed me to move through life with more courage than I could have hoped to possess without it. It is a valuable reminder of language's ability to inspire or to destruct, depending on how we choose to use it, as well as the power of the messages we hold about ourselves. Are there any negative messages that you repeat internally to yourself – something equivalent to my worry that I was too small – and which could be transformed, as mine was, to a more precious jewel?

The other side of this same coin – the negative power of words – was also something I was acutely aware of from an early age. I always aspired to remain a neutral person, never speaking negatively behind my friends' backs, and I believe that this was the key to my ability to enjoy an easy, drama free social life throughout school. I also learned that sometimes, a white lie is more kind than an ugly truth. I am thinking, in particular, of an occasion when I was twelve and a friend, Margaret, gave me a gift. It was one of her own toys – a tatty old doll which had mucky hair and was so unhygienic that it repulsed me. I of course did not share this truth with Margaret, though: it was a sincere gift from her to me and I knew, that was all she had and so I told her I loved it, knowing that it was more important to make Margaret smile than to stick doggedly to the truth.

As for the academic side of school life, I was content that things were ticking along nicely. I regularly came top of my class in tests, including my mock CSEs. Due to the high number of students in our school for whom English was a second language, no one sat O Levels: students were instead able to sit up to a maximum of six CSEs. While the whole year group was entered for Maths and English, only few others and I entered the Biology exam. Even this fact – being one of the few students able to sit six CSEs – gave me confidence that I was thriving academically.

However, when I received my results that August, it became clear that the reality was far less rosy than I had imagined. When I stared at the piece of paper bearing my results and saw that I had completely failed all of my CSEs, I couldn't quite believe my eyes. How could this be?! I had never struggled with the content of my lessons and I had always outstripped my peers in terms of English fluency. Surely these facts alone were enough evidence that I was succeeding? It had never occurred to me that the teachers might have been setting work that did not meet the challenge of the CSEs. It was a truly sobering wake-up call about the narrowness of my horizons.

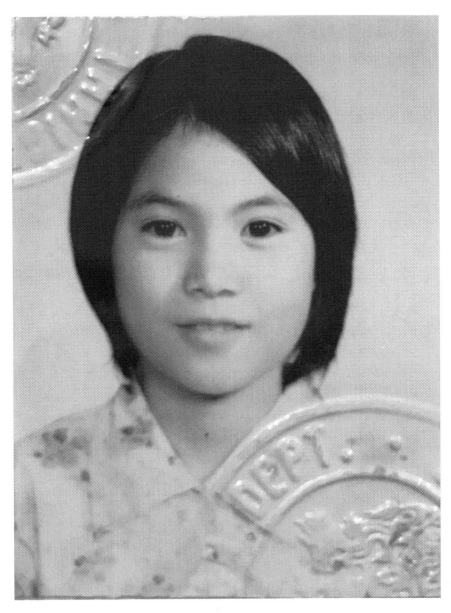

My first passport photo taken before we moved to England.

4

THE COLLEGE YEARS

W hat followed was a period of intense introspection and reflection. As was the case with my peers, I had never dreamed of being any kind of professional when I grew up: I had simply contended myself with moving through life taking it day by day. It was, I suppose, a relatively sheltered existence. We had simply looked forward to finishing school and beginning work, believing this simple progression to be liberating in itself. I had assumed I would begin working in my parents' takeaway. But for some reason, by failing my CSEs, it was as though the comfortable bubble had burst. I was fifteen years old, I had finished school and no qualifications. I thumbed through leaflets for Bourneville, Sutton Coldfield and Matthew Boulton College, but all of them required three CSEs as a minimum for entry. Instead, I went straight to work, alternating between shifts on a counter in a takeaway and as a waitress in a restaurant belonging to a friend of my parents.

Suddenly, the world seemed very small. Day in, day out, I ruminated on the fact that I had no prospects, and the burden of failure weighed heavily on me. As September approached, I thought gloomily of all of the people that would be heading on to college in the weeks that followed. I felt as though I were trapped in a dead end and, somehow, as though I was both lost and trapped at the same time.

It was on one of the evenings following my exam results, as I was working in the takeaway and feeling despondent about the state of my life, that a customer offered me a glimmer of hope. We were chatting about my prospects and I had mentioned my failed CSEs when the customer told me about Solihull College. Apparently, they would allow me to retake my CSEs alongside my further studies.

I distinctly remember the spark of joy that I felt upon hearing this information. It was as though the customer had thrown me a lifeline; I was so excited, and called the college the very next day to confirm what the customer had told me. They said that yes, it was true, and by the next morning an application form had arrived in the post. I was buzzing with excitement at this point, and by the following morning I had completed the form in full and returned it to the college. Within a week of placing the phone call, I had earned a place at Solihull College, and my future looked bright once more!

By this point, my parents had moved again to run a new business – a fish and chip shop, this time, with a small kitchen from which my dad could cook Chinese food. Our new address was quite far from Solihull, but this fact was not enough to dampen my excitement. Every weekday, I would leave the house at 7am, walk for ten minutes, catch a forty-five minutes bus into Birmingham, walk across town to Moor street, catch a twenty minutes train to Solihull and then walk another ten minutes to the college in order to arrive to my lessons by 9am. In spite of the epic scale of this journey, I was always on time and I always arrived with a sense of joy and gratitude in my heart. I truly loved college: I remember vividly how clean and new everything looked, and the feeling of optimism and potential that that gave me. I wandered through the halls on that first day, admiring the tidiness and the freshness of the paint, with great excitement. That day, hearing the crisp, well-spoken voices of my teachers and marvelling at the extent of their expertise, I knew that my life was looking up.

Perhaps the most valuable thing about my time at college was that it opened my eyes to new possibilities, and a world much larger than the one I had existed in so far. Having spent my time living in deprived places like Small Heath and Selly Park, I had become accustomed to a certain level of shabbiness and had never imagined that things could be any different. But as I began to make friends at college, I was repeatedly amazed by how modern their clothes were, by the gorgeous jewellery that the girls wore and the fact that some of them could even drive cars. One of the girls had a white sports car, while another would occasionally pick us up in his sports car in order to take us to McDonalds! I absorbed all of these novelties with quiet amazement, and told myself that one day, just like my new friends, I would be a rich person with beautiful things!

One day near the end of the second term, I was in the dinner hall when a Chinese girl approached me. She introduced herself as Jane, and asked me why she hadn't seen me around the area before. I was struck by her confidence and self-assurance, and noted that this was perhaps another benefit of being wealthy and well-educated. When I told Jane that I didn't live in Solihull, she was shocked: she had lived there all of her life and didn't know anything else. In this respect, I suppose, we were equal: her wealth of everything and my lack of it had been equally sheltering. Jane invited me to join her and her friends for a day out that Sunday. I jumped at the opportunity: having moved around so much, I had found it hard to hold on to a consistent friendship group. Luckily, Jane embraced me into her group and we remain friends to this day!

College continued to be a wonderful environment for me. I re-sat my CSEs and actually did well the second time. It became clear that my struggle had largely been down to the quality of the teaching I had experienced in my school years. I remain ever grateful for the opportunity that I had to try again. Years later, I bumped into a friend I'd known from my school. She was working as a cleaner in a hospital, which left me wondering how different my own life might have been if I hadn't talked to the customer who recommended Solihull College and found my path towards brighter things. This is just one of the many occasions in my life that could be attributed to the support of Gabriel, the angel on my shoulder.

With a handful of CSE passes secured, I moved on to A Level study. I decided on Sociology, Psychology and Statistics, and became utterly fascinated by my studies. Suddenly, I was surrounded by friends with lofty career ambitions: they all hoped to pursue high flying careers as solicitors, professional sports persons and accountants, and had clear visions of what they needed to do to get there. Surrounded by such ambition, I developed a dream of my own. I hoped to study Psychology at university, with a view to working as a psychologist in prisons. For a while, I felt very clearly that I was exactly where I was supposed to be. I had amazing teachers, fabulous friends and I was fascinated with my studies.

It seemed though, that the universe had other plans for me...

5

FIRST LOVE AND
FINDING THE ONE

Those new plans came in the form of a dashing character named Bobby. I remember with perfect clarity the first moment that I saw him: he was skating on an ice rink and I was totally mesmerised. I wasn't the only one: all the girls around him seemed to be going weak at the knees looking at Bobby, and Bobby seemed to be aware of it. He was practically posing in the middle of the ice. Looking back now, he was almost a caricature of a romantic hero: he was well dressed and well spoken, with a chiselled jaw and a charismatic demeanour. I don't remember how it happened, but somehow, Bobby asked me out on a date. All I can recall is that I said yes, I turned up late and the rest is history.

As we are apt to do at that age, I became instantly besotted with Bobby. He quickly became my number one priority, and I left my friendship group behind in favour of Bobby's – a far more rebellious gang who were more interested in disco music than A Levels. Quickly, my own priorities changed too. Much to my parents' frustration, I lost interest in my collegework completely and was instead obsessed with going to discos every weekend (and sometimes, midweek too) with Bobby and his friends. I felt that if I missed even a single event, I would be missing out. Naturally, my studies suffered and, sadly, I dropped out of Solihull College. My mum took to banning me from going out and, in time, I had to end the relationship.

Being young and foolish, I was convinced that the breakup would be temporary, believing that once I had found a way to finish my A Levels, Bobby and I would reunite. Imagine my devastation, then, when Bobby moved on almost immediately. Within a few months of our separation, not only did he have a new girlfriend, but she was pregnant, and they were due to get married a few months later. It was my first experience of heartbreak and it cut deeply. The fact that there was a baby involved made it clear to me that there would be no going back: Bobby and I were history.

On the night of Bobby's wedding, I sat at home, despairing, as the phone rang and rang. Various friends were calling me to check how I was, asking if I was okay, horrified that Bobby could move on so quickly with someone else. I tried to play it cool, thanking my friends for the kind gesture but reassuring them that I was okay and happy for Bobby and his new beau. I must confess though that once the phone stopped ringing, I fell to the ground and sobbed. I even grabbed the phone in a moment of desperation, intending to call Bobby and tell him how much I missed him. I would tell him that he was making a mistake: he should be with me instead. In that moment though, something inexplicably strange happened. I couldn't remember Bobby's number. I knew it off by heart and had called it hundreds of times, but when I went to dial, the numbers wouldn't come to me. Again, this is a moment that I attribute to my guardian angel protecting me: it was as though there was a block in my brain, and it remained there until the feeling of desperation – and my desire to call Bobby – had faded. I spent the whole of the next day lying in bed, waiting for the storm to pass.

In time, things gradually began to go back to normal. Sadly though, my time with Bobby had left me with no enthusiasm for my studies. I attempted to retake my A Levels at West Bromwich – a college much closer to home – but I couldn't seem to summon the enthusiasm for learning that I had felt when starting at Solihull College. For one thing, I was two years older than my peers: my younger brother Alan was even in my class with me. This wasn't the only problem though: for some reason, the information that I was learning just wouldn't seem to stick in my head. I blamed everything and everyone – my environment; my teachers; my peers. Whatever it was, I felt sure that I was wasting my time, and I dropped out.

Thinking that perhaps it might have been West Bromwich that was the problem, I reapplied to Solihull in the hopes that I might regain some of the enthusiasm that the building had inspired in me two years earlier. I managed one term there, but my hopes had not been realised. Seeing that same environment again - but this time, without any of my friends – made me feel incredibly lonely. Instead, I went back to working in a restaurant and attended an evening class at Matthew Boulton College instead. I felt that if I could just pass my A Levels then I'd be able to earn a place at university and move on with my life. But this evening class wasn't the answer either: I just couldn't make the information stick in my head. It seemed as though – no matter what I tried – I couldn't find within me the optimism and love of learning that I had once felt so keenly. To be truthful, at this point in my life, I was unhappy. I felt directionless and, as I had done upon failing my CSEs, trapped by my circumstances.

One day around that time, a close friend of mine, Janet, attempted to cheer me up my setting me up on a blind date. Janet was always inviting me out to lunch or out in the evening, and to whom I was always saying 'no'. On reflection, I suppose I was a little depressing and was burying myself away from the world. Eventually, the friend wore me down and I said yes. It was no use though; the blind date was a failure. My friend was baffled – she was convinced she'd found my perfect match.

'Why don't you like him? He's not much different to the old one! He's tall and handsome!' Janet protested.

'I don't know,' I said, 'maybe it's his hair.'

Janet seemed to get the message and drop the issue, but she was persistent in her attempts to pull me out of my emotional slump. Two weeks later, she convinced me to go out for lunch with her. Lo and behold, I arrived to lunch to find my blind date had accompanied Janet. What's more, he was smartly dressed in a white shirt and well fitted black trousers, and was sporting a new hairstyle!

Touched by Janet's kind efforts, I thanked her for lunch and promised to give the young man another chance.

six weeks later, my blind date and I were engaged! Over the course of those six weeks, Sang had melted my heart: he may have been tall and handsome like Bobby but the similarities ended there. He was also responsible and much more mature than the typical nineteen year old: after taking me to his place of work and impressing me with his culinary skills, I came to respect and trust Sang.

Sang proposed to me while we sat at the dinner table with my parents. His asking them for my hand in marriage was the first I knew of the idea! Although it had only been six weeks something about our relationship just felt right. We were married after only five months. Thirty-two years later, I feel confident that I made the right choice!

Sang and I in Zakynthos 2018

6

TREADING WATER

After we were married, Sang and I lived with my parents and two younger brothers. Two years later, I became pregnant with our first child, meaning that there was seven of us under one roof!

Having Dannielle, our baby daughter, to take care of, I stopped working and relied instead on Sang's income from his work in a restaurant in Streetley, Sutton Coldfield. It wasn't much, but it was enough for us to get by.

During this time, I became somewhat despondent. On one hand, I had a good life. I had a roof over my head and food to eat. I had the support of my parents and a loving, reliable husband. I had a beautiful baby daughter, who made me light up whenever I looked into her eyes. Yet something was undeniably missing. In spite of all of my blessings, I felt an emptiness which I couldn't seem to shake.

Perhaps it was that – after the broad sense of optimism and possibility that I had felt when studying in Solihull, my world seemed to have shrunk again. Once more, my horizons didn't stretch far beyond a council estate in West Bromwich. My life stretched out before me and all I could see was day after day spent at my mother's fish and chip shop. It was a distinctly working-class area and my neighbours were helpful and friendly, seemingly happy with their own version of the simple life. I wished desperately that I could be like them, and just enjoy my life for what it was, taking it day by day. For whatever reason, I didn't seem capable of the task.

One memory from around that time sticks in my mind: my best friend Chau-Ling called to tell me that she had passed all of her exams. I was keenly aware that, had things turned out differently for me, I could have been in the same position: graduating from university, with a wealth of opportunities lying at my feet. I was happy for my friend and told her as much, but when I hung up the phone, I burst into tears.

I did my best to hide my sorrow from my family – it didn't seem fair to focus on what I didn't have when I was lucky in so many other ways. Somehow though, my mum picked up on my feelings. Although we were never a particularly tactile family, she approached me and gave me a hug.

'Daughter,' she said, 'maybe one day, you will have success of your own. Look at your cousin Vicky – she's a business owner at twenty-five! Maybe one day soon, that will be you. But also, now, look at your daughter. There is no amount of money or success that could ever replace what you are holding in your arms right now.'

I looked down at Dannielle, who smiled innocently back at me. Suddenly, I found myself bursting into tears, hugging Dannielle more tightly to me. My mother was right, and it is a lesson that I try to remind myself of to this day: as easy as it can be to envy the experiences of others, it is important to remind ourselves of and remain grateful for our own blessings. It is far too easy to take for granted the gifts that life offers us.

However, another voice in the back of my head held on to that other idea of my mother's. Silently, I told myself: I want to be a business owner before I turn twenty-five.

One day around that time, Sang returned from work at the restaurant in Streetley with the news that he had handed in his notice, following a disagreement with a woman who worked in the kitchen. Sang has always been a responsible and reliable person, and so I trusted his decision. Regardless, I was worried. We had a baby to take care of, and now neither of us was earning a penny.

A few weeks later, I overheard Sang talking to a friend on the phone about a job in Harborne at a restaurant called Henry Wong. The friend was telling Sang that the wage was extremely low, and so he wouldn't be going for it: he would rather not work at all than accept such low pay. When Sang hung up the phone, I implored him to give the job a chance.

'What do you have to lose?' I asked him. 'Even if the wage is low, you aren't working at all as it is, so you aren't sacrificing anything!'

Sang agreed that – until he found something better – it was worth calling up and enquiring. When he did so, the restaurant were interested and asked him to come in for an interview. Luckily, the restaurant that Sang had worked in in Streetley had an excellent reputation, and so when Sang and I visited Henry Wong, they offered him a job then and there. Just like that, we were back on our feet.

After having been so hesitant about the job in the first instance, Sang would go on to enjoy his time at Henry Wong and work there for two years. For a while, life was simple and stable: Sang worked to support us while I took care of Dannielle and focused on counting my blessings.

My Father's 81st birthday. With my Mum
and Brothers. Alan and Tony.

7

BUSINESS BOOMING

We were lucky that the job at Henry Wong helped to keep us afloat when money was tight, but by far the greater gift of the experience was that it brought Harborne to our attention. If Sang had not been working at Henry Wong, perhaps we would not have been aware of a Chinese takeaway shop going up for sale on Harborne High Street. It was a busy and expensive street, so when a friend suggested that Sang and I take a look at it, we were sceptical. Rent was notoriously high and we didn't have much money to spare. Out of curiosity more than anything else, we made an appointment and went along to see what all the fuss was about. We never seriously entertained the idea that we might actually end up buying a business.

When we arrived to the appointment, the woman showing us the shop was very friendly. Still, we didn't take the idea seriously: as we had expected, it was completely out of our price range. It was only when the woman suggested a financial arrangement which would require less money upfront that we actually dared to entertain the idea as a serious possibility. Still, we went home and told my parents, expecting them to shut down the idea and point out all of the negatives. In fact, they were extremely positive and encouraging. With the offer of a loan from them and some additional financial support gathered from our extended family, we tentatively approached a bank to enquire about a loan. We received yet more encouragement from the bank manager, who came to visit the shop with us and told us that it was an excellent location. He agreed to the loan and, to our astonishment, we found ourselves suddenly in a position to start out on our own as business owners. And I became a business owner just a few months before my 25th birthday.

Over the months that followed, I found that the emptiness which I had carried around with me for the preceding few years faded away, and was replaced instead with a buzz of excitement and optimism. Sang and I's heads were both fizzing and popping with ideas. We were just so energised by the prospect of putting our own stamp on a business and building something of our own from scratch. Many of our friends were more sceptical, attempting to discourage us from what seemed to them to be a risky prospect. But nothing could dampen our enthusiasm. We dismissed the negativity and trusted our vision.

Emboldened by our ideas, we asked the landlord to give us two months' rent free so that we could close the shop and renovate it. To our great surprise, the landlord said yes. While the building itself was receiving a healthy dose of TLC, Sang and I put our heads together and worked on our concept. We were keen to think carefully about the market; we researched intensively what the market already had to offer, what was already working well in our local area and what we might be able to offer to set ourselves apart from our competitors.

When we eventually settled on our 'unique selling point', we were thrilled with our idea. We decided that we would offer high class, restaurant quality Chinese food with the best possible service, delivered to our customers' door. As run of the mill as this may sound in 2019, in the 1980s, the concept was utterly revolutionary. While our competitors in the Chinese takeaway market were offering chicken chow mein, chicken fried rice and chicken curry, we were offering Szechuan and Peking duck, with ingredients as fresh and authentic as any restaurant in the city. Our quality of service set us apart from our competitors too – we dressed in uniforms reminiscent of high class restaurants and offered a delivery service for just £1, in the hopes that our customers would feel that the Chinese restaurant experience had been brought into their own home without their having to lift a finger. As hard as it may be to believe today, at the time, we were the only Takeaway shop in the whole of Birmingham that offered such a service. In a sense, the ubiquity of the concept in 2019 is a flattering reflection of the strength of our idea!

We approached our first day of trading with eager anticipation and butterflies in our stomachs. As it turned out though, we had nothing to fear: our concept had got people talking and the shop was packed, with people queuing out the door. In fact, we even ran out of food and had to close up early, sending some hungry customers away!

For seven years, we continued trading from that same takeaway; in all that time, business never slowed down. More than anything, I would put our success down to the clarity of our vision and the high standards we maintained in achieving that vision. From those early days before we'd so much as opened our doors, we knew that our name would be synonymous with high quality food and high quality service. By keeping this simple idea in mind, our customers always knew what to expect from us, and were never disappointed. One example from our early days stands out: we delivered to a man who, when we arrived with our delivery, was dressed from head to toe in traditional Japanese dress. His wife was dressed in a similar fashion, and their dining table was beautifully laid in preparation for the food's arrival. To me, this domestic scene perfectly encapsulated the hopes and dreams we had aspired towards.

We were proud of what we had achieved in such a short time, and that emptiness – which in retrospect could be described as unfulfilled ambition – was certainly sated, we were exhausted, too. Besides working relentlessly on maintaining our standards and meeting the high demands of our business, we were raising a growing family. After Dannielle, Sang and I had two sons – Myles and Jamie. Ultimately, our success at work came at a price: every moment spent working for our business was a moment that we couldn't spend at home with our small children.

After seven crazy years, we were utterly exhausted and ready for a change. For a long while, people had been practically queueing up to buy our business from us, and so it was easy to find a buyer to rent to. Doing so allowed us to buy a new shop and to build up a new business, but this time our reputation allowed us to do so without the added pressure of delivery. Life became calmer, and we were able to slow down and focus more on family life.

Although our venue had changed and we no longer delivered, everything else about our business stayed more or less the same. We used high quality ingredients to make high quality dishes, and this ensured that our new takeaway soon established an excellent reputation of its own. Happily, it was a reputation that would last for twenty years, until we contentedly hung up our aprons and decided that it was time to move on to a new challenge: retirement.

I learned a lot in those first seven years of business. Most of all, I found that it was important to be focused: a business owner must know precisely what service it is that they provide to their customer. Once you have that idea in mind, you must be prepared to work at it! Having a positive attitude and a passion for your product will help here: it will mean that slaving away to achieve your goal will feel like a labour of love, and not just labour.

Once you have got started on your great idea and begun to commit to it, keeping faith is essential. You must believe in your product, so that you are not tempted to give up when the going gets tough. This doesn't mean that you should believe in your product so relentlessly that you don't take feedback into consideration. In fact, quite the opposite. You should see every bit of feedback – whether good or bad – as an opportunity to learn, grow and improve. If you followed the first step and made sure you truly understood what is was that you wanted to offer to your customers, then being adaptable will not compromise your vision; it will only refine it.

I also learned that a successful business is founded on strong relationships, both with one's staff and one's customers. Never forget that your business cannot exist without either of these elements. By treating your customers with honesty and respect, you will build a relationship founded on trust. When it comes to staff, I believe in becoming part of the team. If you treat the team well, they will treat you well in return. This latter point is particularly important, as by developing a team that you can trust, you will gradually be able to delegate, reduce your own input and allow your business to thrive independently from you.

I have always thought of my businesses as being my children: by placing a great deal of effort and love into helping them develop in the early stages, they will gradually grow and become more independent. Over time, the business will be more able to take care of itself, and you will find yourself with more time and freedom for yourself.

My team at work.

8

BALANCING A FAMILY

Dannielle was six when we were able to move into a family home of our own in Harborne, much nearer to our business. After years of penny pinching and relying on my parents to put a roof over our head, it was a wonderful feeling to be building a home and family of our own. Not only that, but the success of our business allowed us a financial freedom that my own parents had never known.

When we first came to Harborne, we lived in the flat above our shop, right in the heart of the high street. We enrolled Dannielle at Station Road School, which was just a three minute walk away. We were incredibly lucky to earn a place: it was a well renowned school, often applied to by parents who would've otherwise sought private education for their children. At that point in my life, private school had not so much as crossed my mind; I was grateful that Dannielle had a place at a respected school so close to home (perhaps another blessing from angel Gabriel?) and didn't think much more into it.

When Dannielle was five, we welcomed our first son, Myles, to the world. And two and a half years later, Jamie followed. Taking care of three young children while running a business would have been more or less impossible had it not been for the support of our live-in nanny, Yin. While we were ferrying food from the takeaway to the homes of our customers, our nanny was able to ferry our children from home to school to after school clubs and back again.

At the time, I was so focused on work that I didn't stop to contemplate the things that I might be missing out on: such small pleasures as reading with my children and putting them to bed sadly passed me by. One evening though, the things that I was missing suddenly became clear to me. I returned home from work and saw Dannielle at the top of the stairs with our nanny. She was dressed in her pyjamas which, I noticed, were far too short in the leg.

'Hello, mummy.' Dannielle said, shyly clinging to her nanny's leg.

Dannielle looked scared. A pang of sorrow filled my heart as I realised that my own little girl didn't know me well enough to feel comfortable in my presence.

'Why are her pyjamas so short?' I snapped at the nanny. 'Have you shrunk them in the wash?'

With the benefit of hindsight, it is clear to me that I was taking out my hurt on the nearest person, but at the time, I was filled with what felt like legitimate frustration.

'No!' She replied, her arm wrapped around Dannielle who still clung protectively to her leg. 'Those are just her pyjamas!'

Staring up at the pair of them from the bottom of the staircase, a moment of clarity descended on me. Without realising, I had become so focused on my work that I had literally missed my daughter growing up. If I had missed that physical growth, what emotional moments of growth had I missed too? Focused as I was on the busy life of a successful businesswoman, what memories of home life had I missed out on?

Without another moment of hesitation, I put down my bags, raced to the top of the stairs and swept Dannielle into my arms.

The sweetness of that hug sticks in my memory to this day: it was a significant moment of realisation for me. As I put Dannielle to bed that night, savouring the moment of bonding with my daughter, I knew that I had learned an important lesson: sometimes in life, we are so busy striving for more that we forget to focus on and be grateful for the gifts that we already possess.

It was around this point that Sang and I sought to slow down our work lives in order to be more involved at home.

It is perhaps worth mentioning at this point that, largely due to my status as a second generation Chinese immigrant, my parenting style is something that I have developed through experience as opposed to by design, and many of the things that have become important to me as a mother are based on lessons learned along the way. I attribute this to my experience as a second generation Chinese immigrant in particular because the difference between the lifestyle and opportunities that my parents had in comparison to mine is vast. When they arrived in the UK in the 1970s, as was the case with many first generation Chinese immigrants at that time, their primary hope for their children was financial security. The typical expectation of a child of my generation was to go to school, to help out in the family business and to one day grow up and work in a takeaway. Focusing on these goals, in a new land with a new language, was a broad enough goal. Since my parents – and many of their peers – had arrived to the UK as adults, they did not adopt the language as easily as their children, and so did not become as immersed in their new culture as we were able to.

By contrast, my generation was able to become part of the fabric of our new country. We went to school with English children, we spoke the language and interacted with English people on a daily basis, from a much younger age. This allowed our horizons to be broader: we were able to see first-hand the things beyond a wage that English people filled their lives with, and this allowed us to aspire for those things too. Just as my peers at Solihull College had allowed me to long for finer clothes, fancy cars and to stay up all night dancing in discos, my fellow parents allowed me to see that a good education meant much more than just sending your child to school.

Since Dannielle's school was so prestigious, the parents that I was mingling with at the school gate were often doctors and solicitors with high aspirations for their children's futures. It was through these interactions that I learned that it was typical to hire a tutor for your children by the age of five, to send them to Kumon classes and to arrange piano or violin lessons for them in their free time. At first, I was sceptical: as I mentioned earlier in this book, by the age of five, I was playing barefoot on the beach on Lantau Island! I had believed that my children needed to worry about little more than colouring in between the lines at age five. However, I also wanted Dannielle to be able to fit in with her classmates, and to have hobbies in common with them. I took the approach of enrolling my children in whatever classes other parents seemed to be enrolling their children in. I truly was learning what parenting meant to me 'on the go'; the more that I learned about the ambitions that other parents had for their children, the greater my own ambitions became.

One Saturday, Dannielle and I were spending time together at home, when I asked her what she had been up to at school the day before.

'Nothing really,' Dannielle told me. 'Except I took the new girl around school. She's just arrived from Iceland.'

'Really?' I asked, confused. 'Weren't you supposed to be in lessons?'

'The teacher said it was ok,' Dannielle replied. 'They said I could miss lessons to spend time with her and help her to settle in.'

I suppose it was a positive thing in some ways: they had trusted Dannielle to be an ambassador for the school and to warmly welcome their newest student. But I was furious. I rang the school immediately and made an appointment with Dannielle's teacher.

'Don't worry Mrs Lam,' the teacher reassured me, smiling kindly. 'We chose Dannielle because she is already so far ahead the rest of the class. In fact, she has already reached the national standard for her age group: we aren't concerned at all about her falling behind.'

Undoubtedly, this response was designed to reassure me. Instead, it only set my mind into panic mode. Surely, I thought, there should not be an arbitrary line of achievement, beyond which we give up on stretching our children? If we cut off our children's success at a fixed, universal line, how can they ever aspire to reach new places and to improve our understanding of what is possible? Perhaps I was afraid that Dannielle would be let down by her school's low expectations of her in the same way that I had, when being top of the class had resulted in a handful of failed CSEs. Or perhaps, having gone from being a barefoot child without an education in Lantau to a successful business owner in Harborne, I had a greater understanding than Dannielle's teachers about the importance of being stretched and having broad horizons.

From then on, for all of my children, I became focused on ensuring that they had access to the best possible education. For me, this meant private school, where I believed the children would receive a more challenging education while mingling with children whose parents had equally high standards for them. I thought back to my friends in school and how their lack of aspirations had allowed me to drift through school without aspirations too, and the confused, unfulfilled years that had followed. I was determined that my own children would experience no such thing.

At the ages of two and three respectively, I enrolled the boys at Holy Child School (now Priory School): the best private school in Edgbaston. By the time they reached Year 3, they were certainly happy and contented, but I feared that they still weren't challenged academically. I moved them to Bluecoat School – a boarding school which I had heard good things about when studying at Solihull College. My hope here was, again, that the boys would mingle with similarly ambitious children. I stopped short of sending them to a prestigious boarding school in Oxford when my younger son asked me, aghast, how I would like it if I had to blow dry my own hair. His skewed perspective on what it meant to be independent left me with the sense that they were too young to live so far from home.

As for Dannielle, she sat entrance exams for five or six different selective secondary schools, and passed every single one of them. Eventually, we decided on King Edwards High School for Girls, as it was private, selective and, of all of her options, had done the best in the league tables. At the time, many of my friends had negative opinions and attempted to dissuade me from sending my children to private school. Although I heard their concerns, I ultimately stayed focused on my own opinions. It is my belief that people will always disagree with you about how you choose to live your life, and sometimes it is important to listen to your own voice. With the benefit of hindsight, I feel that it was one of the best decisions that I have ever made, and that nothing could replace the value of a good education. Now that my children are adults with fulfilling and challenging careers – Dannielle is a Doctor, Jamie is a Veterinary Surgeon and Myles is a Flood and water Specialist – I feel confident that I invested my energy and money in the right way.

There is a great deal of responsibility involved in being a parent: there are so many ways to influence and shape our children's worlds, and sometimes it isn't always clear until afterwards whether our ideas were right or not. My children have always seemed happy – they had a lot of friends and our close proximity to their school meant that many of them regularly dropped in to the house.

I must confess though that I was, in many ways, a strict parent. Perhaps frightened by how distracted from my own path I had been by my relationship with Bobby and the hedonistic friendships which defined that period of my life, I became strict with Dannielle about who she was allowed to socialise with, where she could go and when. I limited her from attending sleepovers at other children's houses, telling her that they were allowed to come to us but that she couldn't go to them. I banned mini-skirts and other revealing clothes, and, even when Dannielle was eighteen, I kept a close eye on her interest in nightclubs.

'You can go out clubbing,' I told her, 'so long as I can pick you up.'

'But what if the night doesn't finish until really late?!' Dannielle protested.

'No matter what time it is, I will be there to pick you up.'

It was in this way that I found myself parked outside of nightclubs at 5 o'clock in the morning, waiting for a frustrated Dannielle who would pile into the backseat while the rest of her friends skipped off to McDonalds for breakfast.

As I mentioned earlier in this chapter, parenthood is something that I – like most parents I suppose – have picked up on the go. Sometimes, I have been happy with these choices; others, less so. Looking back, I worry I was too strict with Dannielle. Although she is certainly academically accomplished, I perhaps did not allow her enough opportunity to 'let loose' as a child, a skill she is trying to teach herself now, as a young adult. Having joined the Royal College of General Practitioners by the age of Twenty-Nine, she is now working as a Doctor while completing a course in lifestyle medicine and, like her mother, training to be a yoga teacher.

Being a parent is a thrilling, demanding and humbling experience. And now, as my children have grown and flourished into adults with full lives of their own, I am humbled still by what I can learn from them, and by how their lives and experiences so vastly exceed what I could ever have dreamed of, when I myself was a little girl on the island of Lantau.

Watching people Lobster Fishing in Florida, USA

A break in Dubai

Horse riding in forte Village in Italy

Snorkeling in Barbados

The Giant tortoises in the Island atoll of Aldabra

Beach in Seychelles, beautiful sand so fine, it
felt like talcum powder beneath our feet

PART TWO

BLOSSOMS

1

LESSONS IN LOVE

I n my fifty years of living, I have met some wonderful men. There was Eddie, the successful businessman who taught me how to behave like a grown-up, and Ming, who taught me what a true gentleman looks like, and Gary, a former Aston Villa football player, who taught me that I'd rather not play second fiddle to someone's illustrious career!

However, as is the case for most people, some of my early experiences of romance were not so wonderful. Besides my first taste of heartbreak with Bobby, my relationship with another man was an early lesson in how painful love can be. My relationship with this person was a classic example of falling in love with someone who was never truly available. There was always an excuse as to why we couldn't be together on his birthday, on Valentine's Day or on New Year's Eve. I knew in my heart that I wasn't his top priority, but something prevented me from standing up for myself, from demanding more or walking away.

One birthday, as usual, his phone was turned off. I sat in bed at home that evening, reading The Times newspaper and wondering where he was, what excuse he would have for me the next day. As I flicked through the pages of the newspaper, my eyes were drawn to a beautiful picture – a painting by Rembrant of a woman in blue silk slippers. I read the attached article, which explained that the picture represented a biblical story in which Jesus offers forgiveness to those who sin. The woman in the picture had been charged with adultery and her community wished to stone her to death by way of punishment. Jesus turned to the baying crowd and said: 'He that is without sin among you, let him first cast a stone at her.' One by one, the crowd disappeared, until it was only Jesus alone with the woman. 'Neither do I condemn thee,' Jesus told her. 'Go and sin no more.'

In that moment, I heard the last few words loud and clear. it was as though a spell had been broken, and a great weight lifted from my shoulders. I knew that my time with this person was over, that I could walk away and learn a lesson from the situation.

As with many areas of life, I believe that every experience of love – either good or bad – carries a lesson within it. Ultimately, we can only move forward in life, but we can do so with the strength that these lessons provide us. Sometimes, our search for love will lead us to pain and trauma. To my mind, this is a good thing. Feelings of sadness are an opportunity to listen to our minds and bodies: if we listen closely enough, we will understand what it was that hurt us, and we will learn to walk away from the situation and never return to it. It is only by being disrespected and sidelined by dishonesty for example, that I learned the importance of mutual respect in romantic relationships. Through pain, we evolve, and bring ourselves closer to happiness and peace.

In the meantime, while you work through your sadness and suffering, listening to your body may help you to identify what you need to feel better. Perhaps you have pent up frustration and need to go for a walk outside. Maybe you feel isolated and need to talk to a friend. Maybe you feel low in mood, and need to listen to music that will make you want to dance; maybe you feel stressed and need to listen to peaceful music to soothe your soul. Sooner or later, your heart will have healed and you will be ready to return to the battlefield of romance, this time armed with a greater understanding of what you need from relationships, as well as greater resilience in terms of taking care of yourself.

I believe that these lessons are things that we, mostly, must learn for ourselves. However, the most important things that I have learned along the way, and that have helped me to sustain a long and happy marriage with my own husband, are as follows:

1) Treat your man with respect: in doing so, you will teach them the kind of respect you expect from them in return.

2) Look after them, so that they know how to look after you in return.

3) Keep strong communication at the centre of your relationship.

2

LESSONS IN PARENTING

Over the years, I have read articles in various media outlets about three different kinds of parent. As you read the following descriptions, ask yourself which one best describes your personal approach:

Tiger Parent: a term coined by Amy Chua in Hymn of the Tiger Mother, these parents are very strict and place great demands on their children. They push and pressure their children into high achievement through an authoritarian parenting style, and take over their children's internal sense and self-motivation.

Dolphin Parent: these parents value their children's happiness and wellbeing above all else. They are firm but flexible: although they value rules, they value creativity and independence just as much. Interested in fostering a sense of balance in their children's lives, their offspring will be encouraged to be sociable, to enjoy life and to cultivate a happy outlook.

Jellyfish Parent: these parents tend to not set any rules or boundaries at all, letting their children run wild and free. Their children will also be allowed to indulge any and all of their whims and interests, whether by binging on videogames instead of doing homework or eating cake and ice-cream for dinner.

Do any of these styles seem familiar? While there is no right or wrong way to parent, it is generally considered that the 'dolphin approach' is the most balanced, combining the stability of the tiger parent with the freedom of the jellyfish. That isn't to say that finding the balance is easy, though. As hard as running as business has been, the challenges of being a parent have been some of the toughest of my life.

One thing is certain: parenthood is a learning curve. No amount of planning and preparation will allow us to escape the fact that parenting is something we learn to do 'on the job'. Consequently, being adaptable as a parent is essential. As our children grow and change, so too do we as their parents. Life isn't perfect, but adaptability allows us to overcome the mistakes we will inevitably make as parents, and to learn from them.

Another key challenge in parenting is realising that there is no 'right' way to parent. There are, in fact, multiple possible approaches. What's more, no two children are the same, so it isn't always easy to see which approach will suit your child best. Some children, for example, are easily stressed and dislike pressure. Others thrive in the face of a challenge, and become easily bored in the very same environment which might make another child feel overwhelmed. In this simple example alone, it becomes clear that there is no 'one size fits all' approach which will work for every child, and so flexibility is clearly essential.

But is flexibility and adaptability are the only keys to success, how can I offer any specific advice on how to raise a child? Well, although I do firmly believe that children are different and have different needs, I also believe that there are some basic requirements which never change. To explain this idea, I like to think of raising children through the metaphor of planting seeds. When we plant a seed, we may well not know what kind of plant it will become; whether it will produce fruit and flowers. Regardless, in order to flourish, the seed would require soil, water and sunlight. Similarly, every child should flourish with stability, nourishment and love. This is the point at which adaptability becomes essential. If a seed grows into a yellow rose, there is no sense in trying to turn it into a pink rose by becoming angry or attempting to control or force it. This, surely, would be a recipe for madness. In the case of a yellow rose, it would be wisest to celebrate the beauty of its hue, and to prune and train its branches carefully so that it might bloom as much as possible. The same is true, I believe, when it comes to raising children. As they grow, listen to them. Talk to them. Have real, honest conversations. Ask yourself when they seem happiest, when their minds seem most energised and alert. Use these ideas – not your own preconceived notions – to guide them towards becoming the best version of themselves.

It is at this point that it is important, I feel, to set boundaries. Paying attention to your child will teach you where their potential lies, but you are the one with the life experience to know how they might fulfil that potential. Boundaries and rules will teach them respect for themselves and others, which will be vital to their success in life. It will also teach them self-discipline, which will allow them – with your encouragement – to keep taking steps towards their goals. By giving them this structure and goal oriented mind-set, they will come to see value and purpose in their life; they will understand that short term sacrifice can be important for future success.

In helping to support your child in fulfilling their potential, it is easy to overstep the line: I know that I have been guilty of this, and so have some of my friends. One friend in particular became very anxious about her daughter's GCSE studies, not allowing her to spend time with friends or make any of her own decisions.

'Try and trust your daughter's judgement,' I suggested, attempting to reassure her. 'I know it isn't easy, but just try to relax.'

'Relax?!' She exclaimed. 'How can I relax? If I relax, my daughter's future might end up down the drain!'

My friend's intentions were good, but the ironic reality of her situation was that her attempts to guide her daughter were not only modelling anxious behaviour and creating a stressful environment, they were depriving her daughter of the ability to develop her own independence, which was what she really needed in order to grow. If we keep managing our children's lives forever, they will absorb the message that we do not trust or respect them, and they will carry these messages about themselves internally, as they step out into the wider world. When the time is right, it is essential that we let go of our children and allow them to become their own people.

If I could offer only three pearls of wisdom about how to thrive as a parent, they would be the following:

1) Establish firm and fair boundaries but be prepared to be flexible
2) Communicate clearly and honestly
3) Provide your child with opportunities which will spark their imagination, create a curious mind and allow them to fulfil their potential

Bike Riding in Center Parcs

South Africa

Skiing in Les Arc. France.

3

LESSONS IN
HAPPINESS

Being happy 100% of the time is, surely, an impossibility. After all, we are human beings, made up of cells and complex biological systems. Our hormones and emotional responses are designed to help us survive in a complex and unpredictable world, not to keep us in a permanent state of bliss. However, I believe that there are strategies that, if used, allow us to manage the ebb and flow of our emotions, so that we can increase the number of happy days and our capacity to handle the sad days.

I have named my personal system, which I use to deal with this issue, 'Awakening the Warrior'. Through this phrase, I am referring to the soul which lies within us all. It is the core of our identity and strength, and sometimes we need to remind ourselves that it is within us, and can guide us when we are unsure how to process our emotions and proceed with our lives.

To 'Awaken the Warrior', we need only follow two steps. In doing so, we connect our bodies and minds, and empower ourselves to take control of our emotions. The two steps simply involve asking two questions:

1. What is the emotion that I'm feeling?

Take a few deep breaths as you think about this – doing so is proven to make us feel calmer by reducing our heartrate and stimulating the parasympathetic nerve system. Once you have done this, instead of letting the negative energy sit in the back of your mind, unexamined, get curious about it. Are you feeling stressed and irritable? Are you lethargic, struggling to focus on a task? Are you anxious, nibbling your fingernails down to the quick? Before you can resolve a problem, you must fully understand its nature. When we feel pain, instead of reaching for a painkiller to mask it, we should first ask ourselves why we are feeling pain. Most likely, the solution already lies within us, and we don't need a magic pill at all. Once we have decided what the pain is that we are feeling, it is time to ask the second question.

2. What would it take for my body to feel better?

This second question is key, because there is an undeniable link between the information processed by our brains and the physiological reactions of our bodies. These physical responses are not exclusively positive: how long would a human last if they forgot to eat and didn't feel hunger, or forgot to drink and didn't feel thirst? Long ago, when our ancestors were hunting for their dinner and saw a predator on the horizon, adrenaline would have coursed through their veins, giving them a sense of fear and triggering the 'fight or flight' response.

Nowadays, we humans may not come into contact with animals on the plains of the Savannah, but we do still experience rushes of adrenaline or stress, perhaps in tense meetings at work or in confrontations with our friends and family. Sadly, in our hectic modern lives, we are less connected with the way that these negative feelings manifest themselves in our body; we often let them settle there, feeling the pain but forgetting the source. If we do not take a moment to reflect on why we are feeling stressed, it may burst out of us in destructive ways, such as by lashing out at a loved one or stuffing our face with junk food. Even worse, we may use a painkiller or drug of some sort to squash down the feeling, masking it instead of addressing it, sending ourselves the message that conquering our negative emotions is only possible through external means. It would be far healthier to sit with ourselves and ask: why am I stressed? What happened? Once we have asked this question, we can think about ways to combat that stress. Perhaps, for you, this would mean taking some deep breaths or practising some yoga. For others, the solution may be to take a gentle walk in nature. Yet others may prefer to exhaust themselves with a run on the treadmill. The key though is sitting with our emotions, identifying them and giving our body what it needs to restore the emotional balance.

This is, of course, true for more feelings than just stress. If you are drained, perhaps you need a good night's sleep or simply a glass of water. If you are sad, maybe you need to listen to some upbeat music and dance around your bedroom, or to call a friend who makes you laugh. In all cases, the key is to connect your mind and body. Every time you do so, you will train yourself in the skill of controlling your mood and the actions that follow from it.

Take this example from my own life: recently, my husband and I were able to go on holiday together for the first time. Having had children and a business to keep us busy over the years, we had to wait until our retirement to finally have a holiday alone. I was so excited to experience a romantic getaway, and to relax, just the two of us.

For me, taking a break from reality and our day to day routine was my vision of the ideal holiday. I longed for peace and quiet, the opportunity to 'chill' and to simply 'be' with each other, enjoying a couples holiday for the first time in thirty-two years of marriage.

Sang, however, had other ideas. He spent the entire first day WhatsApping his friends and colleagues back home, more interested in sending them pictures of the scenery than relaxing and enjoying it with his wife.

I became so angry with Sang that I ran away! I hid on another side of the beach, and found myself bursting with rage. I stayed away from my husband for four hours, fuming, contemplating whether it would be possible to jump on the next flight home.

At first I felt that I was doing well – I had avoided making a scene and hadn't shouted. But in time I realised that this was not enough: I was angry and was hiding from my own husband. It was time to 'Awaken the Warrior'.

I took some deep breaths, until I felt some of the tension release from my muscles, and my heartrate began to slow. Once I felt a little calmer, I asked myself: 'what is the pain that I'm feeling?' I knew that I was angry. 'What does my body need to feel better?' I asked. I realised that I needed to understand why. I needed to think about Sang, and why he was behaving the way that he was. Perhaps, I wondered, this is simply his way of showing excitement. It is his first holiday as a couple too. Not everybody finds it relaxing to lie still and do nothing: perhaps his happiness and appreciation of our time together simply looks different to mine.

Having had this conversation with myself, I felt the tension lift almost entirely from my body, and I wanted to see my husband again. I moved from my hiding place and strolled along the beach, where I quickly found Sang. When he saw me, a look of relief spread across his face.

'I've been looking for you everywhere!' He said, holding out his hand. 'Would you like to go for dinner?'

I took his hand, feeling joy surging through my body. I realised that he did appreciate me and wanted to be away with me, he had just expressed himself in a different way. It all became clear, as soon as I had given myself time to understand it.

'Thank you,' I said to my warrior, as I walked along the beach, ready to enjoy a peaceful dinner with Sang.

As in this example of my holiday with Sang, sometimes you may be feeling sad because of negative thoughts that are swirling through the back of your mind, unacknowledged. In these situations, I still believe that it is important to 'Awaken the Warrior' and to listen to your thoughts. Usually, you will hear your thoughts telling you something unpleasant. Perhaps, for example, you went shopping, and for the rest of the day, you have been quietly telling yourself: 'I couldn't fit into those size 8 jeans earlier; I'm so fat and disgusting.' If you listen to yourself and hear a thought like this, it is important to talk back to yourself.

'Your body is just your vessel, like a house or a car, and in that way it has served you well. It is healthy and strong and beautiful and has supported you through thick and thin. Fitting into a pair of size 8 jeans does not make you any more or less worthy of feeling happy and peaceful in this moment.'

It might seem silly to have conversations with yourself, but remember that you are already having conversations with yourself: it's just that the conversation so far has been quite negative. Science suggests that happy thoughts result in the release of endorphins (happy hormones) in the brain. Thus, by taking control of your inner dialogue with more positive thoughts, you can literally train your brain to become a happier place. This does not mean that you should ignore bad thoughts and pretend that they don't happen: in fact, it means quite the opposite. Listen to the negative thoughts and reframe them by looking for reasons to be grateful.

As with negative thoughts about yourself, I believe that it is important to eliminate negative thoughts about others from your mind. Try not to gossip about other people or to hold onto grudges:

both are easy ways of building up a negative picture of the world around you and the people that fill it. By inwardly forgiving people for ways that you have felt wronged, and by not indulging in negative conversations about others, you will continue to ensure that the world in which you exist remains a positive and beautiful one.

Be patient, and if you are consistent in these approaches, you will find that your mind becomes a happier place to be, and that you are more capable of dealing with the times when you feel unhappy.

Christmas in Whistler Village. Canada

Dannielle joining The Royal College of
General Practitioners (RCGP)

Jamie's Graduation

My beautiful family

4

MINI LESSONS

Below are a selection of miscellaneous tips and tricks, picked up along my own journey of life, which I believe to be useful in living a happier life.

- You are the leading lady of your life and the writer of your own story. What story do you want to tell with your precious life?
- Close friends are the most precious jewels in the jewellery box of your life. You do not need more than a handful of true friends, but you should treat that handful of jewels as your most treasured possession. My best friends, Alison and Charlene, are worth more than their weight in gold for the love and support that they bring to my life.
- Eat what you enjoy, but remember that wholesome food will nourish you more deeply than a piece of cake. Do your own research and you will discover that food can be its own medicine cabinet: Brazil nuts contain selenium, pumpkin seeds contain magnesium and dark chocolate contains

polyphenols, all of which are known to have a positive effect on mood.

- Give yoga a try: it is a perfect way to awaken the energy throughout your body and mind, and to relax the nervous system.

- Always remember that tomorrow is a new day; no matter how many mistakes you may make, there is always an opportunity to start again.

- When it comes to exercise, listen to your body and do what you enjoy. Don't go to the gym if you hate it: find a sport or a YouTube workout that works for you instead. The main aim is to challenge yourself and work up a sweat.

- Find a creative hobby – whether that's knitting, reading or writing a blog – that matters to you.

- There is no 'one size fits all' approach in life; everyone's circumstances are different, so the most important thing is to put processes in place which work for you and your life.

EPILOGUE

Final Thoughts

I truly believe that our thoughts affect how we move through the journey of our life. On that fateful day in the fields of Glastonbury, Elona Woods called it Gabriel - an angel sitting on my shoulder. Maybe she was right, maybe it was spiritual nonsense. In either case, I have always found in my own life that if I tell myself of a goal or a wish in life, someone, somewhere – whether an angel, a God or the universe itself – has been listening. They have heard the whisper of my thoughts and have laid a path for me to follow; in following it, I have been led through a life which has allowed me to reach my dreams.

The thing about life is that it will happen to us, whether we want it to or not. We need only look to nature to see the truth in this statement. The flowers that grow from the earth, the bees that pollinate them and every other expression of nature in between: all of them live a life effortlessly. They don't need to be told what colour their petals should be, or why they should be interested in pollen. They are born with all the knowledge and instinct they need to keep themselves alive. We, as human beings, are the same. We have our minds, our beautiful and complex inner worlds. Our mind is a seed which – if we only nurture it with the right thoughts – will blossom beyond our wildest dreams.

Printed in the United States
By Bookmasters